RECORDER

101 DISNEY SONGS

Available for
FLUTE, CLARINET, ALTO SAX, TENOR SAX, TRUMPET,
HORN, TROMBONE, VIOLIN, VIOLA, CELLO, RECORDER,
BELLS/GLOCKENSPIEL

ISBN 978-1-7051-3726-0

The following songs are the property of:

Bourne Co.
Music Publishers
5 West 37th Street
New York, NY 10018

BABY MINE
GIVE A LITTLE WHISTLE
HEIGH-HO
HI-DIDDLE-DEE-DEE (AN ACTOR'S LIFE FOR ME)
I'M WISHING
I'VE GOT NO STRINGS
SOME DAY MY PRINCE WILL COME
WHEN I SEE AN ELEPHANT FLY
WHEN YOU WISH UPON A STAR
WHISTLE WHILE YOU WORK
WHO'S AFRAID OF THE BIG BAD WOLF?
WITH A SMILE AND A SONG

Visit Hal Leonard Online at
www.halleonard.com

Contact us:
Hal Leonard
7777 West Bluemound Road
Milwaukee, WI 53213
Email: info@halleonard.com

In Europe, contact:
Hal Leonard Europe Limited
42 Wigmore Street
Marylebone, London, W1U 2RN
Email: info@halleonardeurope.com

In Australia, contact:
Hal Leonard Australia Pty. Ltd.
4 Lentara Court
Cheltenham, Victoria, 3192 Australia
Email: info@halleonard.com.au

CONTENTS

*Based on the "Winnie the Pooh" works,
by A. A. Milne and E. H. Shepard

**TARZAN® Owned by Edgar Rice Burroughs, Inc.
and Used by Permission.
© Burroughs/Disney

BABY MINE
from DUMBO

RECORDER

Words by NED WASHINGTON
Music by FRANK CHURCHILL

Moderately slow

THE BALLAD OF DAVY CROCKETT
from DAVY CROCKETT

Words by TOM BLACKBURN
Music by GEORGE BRUNS

Moderately

BELLA NOTTE

from LADY AND THE TRAMP

Music and Lyrics by PEGGY LEE
and SONNY BURKE

BE OUR GUEST

from BEAUTY AND THE BEAST

RECORDER

Lyrics by HOWARD ASHMAN
Music by ALAN MENKEN

BEAUTY AND THE BEAST

from BEAUTY AND THE BEAST

RECORDER

Lyrics by HOWARD ASHMAN
Music by ALAN MENKEN

Moderately slow

BELLE
from BEAUTY AND THE BEAST

RECORDER

Music by ALAN MENKEN
Lyrics by HOWARD ASHMAN

BIBBIDI-BOBBIDI-BOO
(The Magic Song)
from CINDERELLA

Words by JERRY LIVINGSTON
Music by MACK DAVID and AL HOFFMAN

BREAKING FREE
from HIGH SCHOOL MUSICAL

RECORDER

Words and Music by
JAMIE HOUSTON

Moderately

BEST OF FRIENDS
from THE FOX AND THE HOUND

RECORDER

Words by STAN FIDEL
Music by RICHARD JOHNSTON

CAN YOU FEEL THE LOVE TONIGHT
from THE LION KING

RECORDER

Music by ELTON JOHN
Lyrics by TIM RICE

Pop Ballad

CANDLE ON THE WATER

from PETE'S DRAGON

RECORDER

Words and Music by AL KASHA
and JOEL HIRSCHHORN

CHIM CHIM CHER-EE

from MARY POPPINS

RECORDER

Words and Music by RICHARD M. SHERMAN
and ROBERT B. SHERMAN

CIRCLE OF LIFE
from THE LION KING

RECORDER

Music by ELTON JOHN
Lyrics by TIM RICE

Moderately (with an African beat)

THE CLIMB
from HANNAH MONTANA: THE MOVIE

RECORDER

Words and Music by JESSI ALEXANDER
and JON MABE

CRUELLA DE VIL
from 101 DALMATIANS

RECORDER

Words and Music by
MEL LEVEN

A DREAM IS A WISH YOUR HEART MAKES
from CINDERELLA

Words and Music by MACK DAVID,
AL HOFFMAN and JERRY LIVINGSTON

FEED THE BIRDS
(Tuppence a Bag)
from MARY POPPINS

Words and Music by RICHARD M. SHERMAN
and ROBERT B. SHERMAN

COLORS OF THE WIND
from POCAHONTAS

RECORDER

Music by ALAN MENKEN
Lyrics by STEPHEN SCHWARTZ

DO YOU WANT TO BUILD A SNOWMAN?

from FROZEN

RECORDER

Music and Lyrics by KRISTEN ANDERSON-LOPEZ
and ROBERT LOPEZ

DAYS IN THE SUN

from BEAUTY AND THE BEAST

RECORDER

Music by ALAN MENKEN
Lyrics by TIM RICE

Moderately

EVERMORE
from BEAUTY AND THE BEAST

Music by ALAN MENKEN
Lyrics by TIM RICE

RECORDER

HEIGH-HO
(The Dwarfs' Marching Song)
from SNOW WHITE AND THE SEVEN DWARFS

Words by LARRY MOREY
Music by FRANK CHURCHILL

Brightly, cheerfully

FOR THE FIRST TIME IN FOREVER

from FROZEN

RECORDER

Music and Lyrics by KRISTEN ANDERSON-LOPEZ
and ROBERT LOPEZ

Moderately, with excitement

Moderately, with expression

HI-DIDDLE-DEE-DEE
(An Actor's Life for Me)
from PINOCCHIO

Words by NED WASHINGTON
Music by LEIGH HARLINE

FRIEND LIKE ME

from ALADDIN

RECORDER

Lyrics by HOWARD ASHMAN
Music by ALAN MENKEN

Bright Two-beat

GASTON
from BEAUTY AND THE BEAST

RECORDER

Music by ALAN MENKEN
Lyrics by HOWARD ASHMAN

Moderately slow, in 1

GOD HELP THE OUTCASTS

from THE HUNCHBACK OF NOTRE DAME

RECORDER

Music by ALAN MENKEN
Lyrics by STEPHEN SCHWARTZ

GIVE A LITTLE WHISTLE
from PINOCCHIO

Words by NED WASHINGTON
Music by LEIGH HARLINE

Moderately, in 2

GO THE DISTANCE

from HERCULES

RECORDER

Music by ALAN MENKEN
Lyrics by DAVID ZIPPEL

HAKUNA MATATA

from THE LION KING

RECORDER

Music by ELTON JOHN
Lyrics by TIM RICE

HAPPY WORKING SONG

from ENCHANTED

RECORDER

Music by ALAN MENKEN
Lyrics by STEPHEN SCHWARTZ

HE'S A PIRATE

from PIRATES OF THE CARIBBEAN: THE CURSE OF THE BLACK PEARL

RECORDER

Music by KLAUS BADELT,
GEOFFREY ZANELLI and HANS ZIMMER

HE'S A TRAMP
from LADY AND THE TRAMP

Words and Music by PEGGY LEE
and SONNY BURKE

HOW DOES A MOMENT LAST FOREVER

from BEAUTY AND THE BEAST

RECORDER

Music by ALAN MENKEN
Lyrics by TIM RICE

I JUST CAN'T WAIT TO BE KING

from THE LION KING

Music by ELTON JOHN
Lyrics by TIM RICE

Bright Two-beat

HOW FAR I'LL GO

from MOANA

RECORDER

Music and Lyrics by
LIN-MANUEL MIRANDA

Moderately, in 2

I'M LATE
from ALICE IN WONDERLAND

Words by BOB HILLIARD
Music by SAMMY FAIN

Moderately fast

I SEE THE LIGHT

from TANGLED

RECORDER

Music by ALAN MENKEN
Lyrics by GLENN SLATER

Moderately

I'M WISHING

from SNOW WHITE AND THE SEVEN DWARFS

Words by LARRY MOREY
Music by FRANK CHURCHILL

Moderately slow, in 2

I'LL MAKE A MAN OUT OF YOU

from MULAN

RECORDER

Music by MATTHEW WILDER
Lyrics by DAVID ZIPPEL

Moderately

IN SUMMER
from FROZEN

RECORDER

Music and Lyrics by KRISTEN ANDERSON-LOPEZ
and ROBERT LOPEZ

Moderately, in 2

I'VE GOT A DREAM
from TANGLED

RECORDER

Music by ALAN MENKEN
Lyrics by GLENN SLATER

Moderately fast

IF I CAN'T LOVE HER

from BEAUTY AND THE BEAST: THE BROADWAY MUSICAL

RECORDER

Music by ALAN MENKEN
Lyrics by TIM RICE

IF I NEVER KNEW YOU

(End Title)

from POCAHONTAS

RECORDER

Music by ALAN MENKEN
Lyrics by STEPHEN SCHWARTZ

Moderately slow

I'VE GOT NO STRINGS
from PINOCCHIO

RECORDER

Words by NED WASHINGTON
Music by LEIGH HARLINE

IT'S A SMALL WORLD
from Disney Parks' "it's a small world" attraction

Words and Music by RICHARD M. SHERMAN
and ROBERT B. SHERMAN

KISS THE GIRL

from THE LITTLE MERMAID

RECORDER

Music by ALAN MENKEN
Lyrics by HOWARD ASHMAN

LAVA
from LAVA

RECORDER

Music and Lyrics by
JAMES FORD MURPHY

Moderately slow, in 2

LOVE IS AN OPEN DOOR

from FROZEN

RECORDER

Music and Lyrics by KRISTEN ANDERSON-LOPEZ
and ROBERT LOPEZ

LET IT GO

from FROZEN

RECORDER

Music and Lyrics by KRISTEN ANDERSON-LOPEZ
and ROBERT LOPEZ

Slowly, in 2

LAVENDER BLUE
(Dilly Dilly)
from SO DEAR TO MY HEART

RECORDER

Words by LARRY MOREY
Music by ELIOT DANIEL

MICKEY MOUSE MARCH
from THE MICKEY MOUSE CLUB

Words and Music by
JIMMIE DODD

LET'S GO FLY A KITE
from MARY POPPINS

Words and Music by RICHARD M. SHERMAN
and ROBERT B. SHERMAN

With gusto

THE LORD IS GOOD TO ME
from MELODY TIME

RECORDER

Words and Music by KIM GANNON
and WALTER KENT

MY FUNNY FRIEND AND ME
from THE EMPEROR'S NEW GROOVE

Lyrics by STING
Music by STING and DAVID HARTLEY

PART OF YOUR WORLD

from THE LITTLE MERMAID

RECORDER

Music by ALAN MENKEN
Lyrics by HOWARD ASHMAN

Moderately bright

MOTHER KNOWS BEST

from TANGLED

RECORDER

Music by ALAN MENKEN
Lyrics by GLENN SLATER

A PIRATE'S LIFE

from PETER PAN

Words by ED PENNER
Music by OLIVER WALLACE

RUMBLY IN MY TUMBLY
from THE MANY ADVENTURES OF WINNIE THE POOH

Words and Music by RICHARD M. SHERMAN
and ROBERT B. SHERMAN

REFLECTION
from MULAN

RECORDER

Music by MATTHEW WILDER
Lyrics by DAVID ZIPPEL

Moderately slow

THE SECOND STAR TO THE RIGHT
from PETER PAN

Words by SAMMY CAHN
Music by SAMMY FAIN

SEIZE THE DAY
from NEWSIES

RECORDER

Music by ALAN MENKEN
Lyrics by JACK FELDMAN

SO THIS IS LOVE
(The Cinderella Waltz)
from CINDERELLA

RECORDER

Words and Music by MACK DAVID,
AL HOFFMAN and JERRY LIVINGSTON

SO CLOSE
from ENCHANTED

RECORDER

Music by ALAN MENKEN
Lyrics by STEPHEN SCHWARTZ

Moderately slow, in 4

THE SIAMESE CAT SONG
from LADY AND THE TRAMP

RECORDER

Words and Music by PEGGY LEE
and SONNY BURKE

Slowly

SOME DAY MY PRINCE WILL COME
from SNOW WHITE AND THE SEVEN DWARFS

Words by LARRY MOREY
Music by FRANK CHURCHILL

Moderately

SOMEDAY
from THE HUNCHBACK OF NOTRE DAME

RECORDER

Music by ALAN MENKEN
Lyrics by STEPHEN SCHWARTZ

SOMETHING THERE

from BEAUTY AND THE BEAST

RECORDER

Music by ALAN MENKEN
Lyrics by HOWARD ASHMAN

A SPOONFUL OF SUGAR

from MARY POPPINS

RECORDER

Words and Music by RICHARD M. SHERMAN
and ROBERT B. SHERMAN

SUPERCALIFRAGILISTICEXPIALIDOCIOUS

RECORDER

from MARY POPPINS

Words and Music by RICHARD M. SHERMAN
and ROBERT B. SHERMAN

"THIS IS ME."
from RATATOUILLE

RECORDER

Music by MICHAEL GIACCHINO

THAT'S HOW YOU KNOW

from ENCHANTED

RECORDER

Music by ALAN MENKEN
Lyrics by STEPHEN SCHWARTZ

TOYLAND MARCH
from BABES IN TOYLAND

Adapted from V. HERBERT Melody
Words by MEL LEVEN
Music by GEORGE BRUNS

TRASHIN' THE CAMP

(Pop Version)

from TARZAN™

RECORDER

Words and Music by
PHIL COLLINS

THE UNBIRTHDAY SONG
from ALICE IN WONDERLAND

RECORDER

Words and Music by MACK DAVID,
AL HOFFMAN and JERRY LIVINGSTON

TRUE LOVE'S KISS
from ENCHANTED

RECORDER

Music by ALAN MENKEN
Lyrics by STEPHEN SCHWARTZ

WESTWARD HO, THE WAGONS!

from WESTWARD HO, THE WAGONS!

Words by TOM BLACKBURN
Music by GEORGE BRUNS

WE BELONG TOGETHER

from TOY STORY 3

RECORDER

Music and Lyrics by
RANDY NEWMAN

WHEN I SEE AN ELEPHANT FLY

from DUMBO

Words by NED WASHINGTON
Music by OLIVER WALLACE

WE KNOW THE WAY

from MOANA

RECORDER

Music by OPETAIA FOA'I
Lyrics by OPETAIA FOA'I
and LIN-MANUEL MIRANDA

Moderately

A WHALE OF A TALE
from 20,000 LEAGUES UNDER THE SEA

RECORDER

Words and Music by NORMAN GIMBEL
and AL HOFFMAN

With a bounce

WE'RE ALL IN THIS TOGETHER

from HIGH SCHOOL MUSICAL

RECORDER

Words and Music by MATTHEW GERRARD
and ROBBIE NEVIL

WHISTLE WHILE YOU WORK
from SNOW WHITE AND THE SEVEN DWARFS

Words by LARRY MOREY
Music by FRANK CHURCHILL

WHEN SHE LOVED ME

from TOY STORY 2

RECORDER

Music and Lyrics by
RANDY NEWMAN

Tenderly, very freely

WHEN YOU WISH UPON A STAR
from PINOCCHIO

RECORDER

Words by NED WASHINGTON
Music by LEIGH HARLINE

Moderately

WHEN WILL MY LIFE BEGIN?

from TANGLED

RECORDER

Music by ALAN MENKEN
Lyrics by GLENN SLATER

Moderately, in 2

Moderately slow (in 4)

Slowly, freely

WITH A SMILE AND A SONG
from SNOW WHITE AND THE SEVEN DWARFS

Words by LARRY MOREY
Music by FRANK CHURCHILL

Moderately slow, in 2

WHO'S AFRAID OF THE BIG BAD WOLF?

from THREE LITTLE PIGS

RECORDER

Words and Music by
FRANK CHURCHILL
Additional Lyric by ANN RONELL

Moderately, in 2

WINNIE THE POOH

from THE MANY ADVENTURES OF WINNIE THE POOH

RECORDER

Words and Music by RICHARD M. SHERMAN
and ROBERT B. SHERMAN

Tenderly

A WHOLE NEW WORLD

from ALADDIN

RECORDER

Music by ALAN MENKEN
Lyrics by TIM RICE

THE WONDERFUL THING ABOUT TIGGERS

RECORDER

from THE MANY ADVENTURES OF WINNIE THE POOH

Words and Music by RICHARD M. SHERMAN
and ROBERT B. SHERMAN

Very brightly

YO HO

(A Pirate's Life for Me)

from Disney Parks' Pirates of the Caribbean attraction

Words by XAVIER ATENCIO
Music by GEORGE BRUNS

In a robust manner

THEME FROM ZORRO

from the Television Series

Words by NORMAN FOSTER
Music by GEORGE BRUNS

Moderately, in 2

WRITTEN IN THE STARS

from AIDA

RECORDER

Music by ELTON JOHN
Lyrics by TIM RICE

YOU CAN FLY! YOU CAN FLY! YOU CAN FLY!

RECORDER

from PETER PAN

Words by SAMMY CAHN
Music by SAMMY FAIN

YOU ARE THE MUSIC IN ME

from HIGH SCHOOL MUSICAL 2

RECORDER

Words and Music by
JAMIE HOUSTON

Moderately fast Rock

YOU'LL BE IN MY HEART
(Pop Version)
from Walt Disney Pictures' TARZAN™

RECORDER

Words and Music by
PHIL COLLINS

YOU'RE WELCOME
from MOANA

RECORDER

Music and Lyrics by
LIN-MANUEL MIRANDA

ZIP-A-DEE-DOO-DAH
from SONG OF THE SOUTH

Words by RAY GILBERT
Music by ALLIE WRUBEL

ZERO TO HERO
from HERCULES

RECORDER

Music by ALAN MENKEN
Lyrics by DAVID ZIPPEL

Driving 4

YOU'VE GOT A FRIEND IN ME

from TOY STORY

RECORDER

Music and Lyrics by
RANDY NEWMAN